JOSEPH KAYE,

BUILDER, OF HUDDERSFIELD

c.1779 to 1858

Edward J. Law

HUDDERSFIELD LOCAL HISTORY SOCIETY

£1.75

OTHER PUBLICATIONS:

By the Society,

JOHN BENSON PRITCHETT
FIRST MEDICAL OFFICER OF HEALTH FOR HUDDERSFIELD J.B. Eagles £1.50

By the Author

18th CENTURY HUDDERSFIELD
THE DAY - BOOKS OF JOHN TURNER 1732-1773 £2.00

Published by
HUDDERSFIELD LOCAL HISTORY SOCIETY

Printed by
SWIFTPRINT
Wood Street, Huddersfield

CONTENTS

Page

ILLUSTRATIONS

ACKNOWLEDGEMENTS

Grateful thanks are due to Kirklees Libraries, Museums and Arts, Huddersfield Art Gallery, for permission to reproduce the photographs of the two portraits of Joseph Kaye, which were taken by the Royal Commission on the Historical Monuments of England.

JOSEPH KAYE, BUILDER, OF HUDDERSFIELD, c1779 - 1858

Edward J. Law

To say that Joseph Kaye was a builder is an understatement, he was much more, but he was a builder; an extraordinary builder. He may almost be said to have been *the* builder of Huddersfield. In the first sixty years of the nineteenth century when Huddersfield grew from a small market town, little more than a village, to a populous commercial and industrial centre, he was responsible for the erection of between one-third and one-half of the houses, as well as many of the major buildings; churches, chapels. hospital, warehouses and factories. At the peak of his activities he was employing over 1,000[1] men and at one time was simultaneously building six churches!

Little is known of his origins, he was born c.1779, the record of his baptism has not been found, but we know that he was the son of John Kaye, an innkeeper[2].

The records of the Brewsters Sessions[3] throw some light on the family in the last quarter of the eighteenth century. The sessions were held annually before two Justices of the Peace when innkeepers were required to appear in person with one or more sureties who stood to forfeit a fixed sum if the licence holder defaulted on the conditions of the licence. Entries are found for Kayes in each of the surviving Huddersfield lists as follows: -

1771	Kay John snr. Kay John jnr. A Cert	1773	Kaye John snr - unfit to come. Kaye John jnr
1777	John Kaye Sarah Kaye, widow - old.	1778	Sarah Kaye wid. John Kaye
1781	Sarah Kaye wid. Eliz Kaye wid.	1803	Joseph Kaye Wool Pack.

The rent roll of the Huddersfield estate of the Ramsden family for a similar period has the following entries: -

1768/9	John Kay £2
1771/2	John Kay £2 Land now let to John Kaye, mason £9.
1798/9	Kaye John Masons Arms £36. Kaye widow of John Back Green £3.3.0

The information from the Brewsters Sessions would appear to be three generations of the family; the grandparents John (I) and Sarah, he dying between 1773 and 1777, the parents John (II) and Elizabeth, he dying between 1778 and 1781, and the son Joseph. The expected burial entries are to be found in the parish registers: 1.11.1775 John Kaye of Huddersfield, 19.4.1781 John Kaye of Huddersfield. The note against John Kaye jnr in 1771 is significant, a certificate was required where the applicant was a new licence holder.

Similarly the Ramsden rentals may be the same three generations; John (I) paying £2, John (II) the mason paying £9 and John (III), son of John (II) and brother of Joseph, of the Masons Arms, paying £36. The rent of £36 was probably for the same land as that previously held by the father at £9. The Ramsdens do not appear to have increased rentals during a continuing tenancy, being satisfied to review at the time of a change on the basis of the economic situation at that time and the nature of any buildings erected on the leasehold.

The widow of John noted in 1798/9 was not Elizabeth, widow of John (II), she died in December 1785 the burial being noted in the parish registers. It is not impossible that it was Sarah, widow of John (I) who was described in 1777 as old, but is more likely to have been the widow of John Kaye, a butcher, who died in 1778.

• • •

Nothing is known of Kaye's childhood but on the basis of the above assumptions he was an orphan by the age of seven. If they had been left destitute and friendless there is little doubt that he and his brother would have been thrown on the parish. As inmates of the workhouse they would have been placed out as parish apprentices at the earliest opportunity, to some unwilling tradesman forced to accept them by the township officials. However, it seems more likely that they were taken in by relatives and friends. Probably they had been left some money by their parents, and possibly a business or businesses. The description of the father as a mason could well indicate a builder rather than a labourer or quarryhand, and it seems likely that he kept the Masons Arms which his son John Kaye was occupying in 1798. At the same time Joseph had commenced as a builder which may indicate some freedom of choice in following his father's trade.

In the obituary of Joseph Kaye[4] it is stated that he had commenced as a builder in his nineteenth year. If this is taken at face value he must at that time have been learning the trade for a number of years, either as apprentice to a builder or as a labourer on building sites.

That his future success did not come without some hardship is shown by the reminiscences of his grandson, Sir Alfred Kaye Rollit, who stated[5] that Kaye had commenced his work as a mason in Manchester walking there each Monday morning and walking back at the end of the weeks work on Saturday evening.

From the above reminiscences we learn that one of Kaye's first domestic buildings was the house Thornton Lodge. John Horsfall, a Huddersfield merchant, had bought eleven acres of land at Longroyd Bridge in 1792 and added a further nineteen acres in February 1802 at which latter date he was still resident in Huddersfield[6]. He was of the family who had lived for at least 200 years at Well in Huddersfield. Having prospered he was no doubt looking to erect a house more befitting his status than the family home in Beast Market, which was rapidly declining as a residential area. To acquire a freehold estate he had little option but to look outside Huddersfield and must have considered himself fortunate to have acquired an estate on the very edge of the Township.

By June 1804 John Horsfall was described as 'of Thornton Lodge' which would put the erection of the mansion between February 1802 and June 1804. The building still stands, and whilst its aesthetic appeal has been blighted by partitioning and extensions, the fabric is sound and reflects credit on the man who built it over 180 years ago. The building would call for more than basic skills, it does not follow the four-square format of many buildings of the Georgian period, the rounded projections of the front, the mixture of single and double storey and the handsome tower which used to adorn[7] it would all test the ability of the builder.

• • •

One can hardly imagine that Kaye's first commission would be for such a mansion, probably he had been occupied in the five years prior with erecting cottages and housing in and around Huddersfield. No doubt John Horsfall living in the town had observed his operations and the quality of his work and it must have been an indication of his standards and reliability that he was appointed to build Thornton Lodge.

Probably many of the small buildings erected by Kaye came via the money or building clubs which were coming into evidence from the beginning of the nineteenth century; they were the forerunners of the present-day building societies. A number of people would club together, often based on an inn or public house, each taking one or more shares to pay a fixed weekly sum into the club. The clubs functioned in a variety of ways, no doubt according to the initial wishes of the founding members. If the club were purely for housing, then as sufficient funds became available to build a dwelling a ballot or draw would be held to determine which 'shareholder' should benefit. Money clubs did not have the specific objective of providing houses, though no doubt some of their members joined for that purpose; their intent was to provide a capital sum for whatever purpose the individual member had in mind, often it was for use in their trade. In some cases the order in which the members became entitled to their share was by ballot, but in other instances the capital sums were bid for as they became available. A member would write his bid on a piece of paper at the monthly meetings, the highest bidder having the privilege of drawing his share that month.

We have seen that Kaye was at the Woolpack in 1803 and he would have actively encouraged a club, it would have been a source of trade for the house on club nights and must have been of advantage when members were deciding upon the builder of their property. A Woolpack Club is known to have been in existence in 1812[8] when Kaye, wanting money from a client for whom he had built property, paid a member five guineas to dispose of his £100 share to that client! Virtually all property in Huddersfield was built on land owned by the Ramsden estate and they had to be notified of mortgages or other third party interests in buildings if they were to protect the interests of those people. Such were the circumstances in which the following letter was written to the Ramsden's local agent: -

> The sum of money required to pay off the claim of the Woolpack Club (including £11.12.6 for rents in arrears) from the estate or buildings of John Crowther, a bankrupt, amounts to £153.6.11 as a statement in the hands of Mr. Joseph Kay will show and who is impowered to act for the said club instead of
>
> Benjn. Bradshaw
>
> Huddersfield Nov. 6, 1819
> To Jno. Bower Esq.

No doubt the members would have been glad to have had a man of Kaye's standing and business acumen to help in the administration of the club. The clubs were a vehicle for investment, much as the present day building societies, and Benjamin Bradshaw, the signatory to the above letter, was a surgeon, a friend and neighbour of Kaye; some years later his son was to marry Kaye's daughter.

The combination of the activities of builder and publican were to continue to be successfully associated by Kaye for the remainder of his life.

The Land Tax return for 1803[9], the first year in which Kaye is noted at the Woolpack shows that Thomas Mills paid 1/7d in respect of the Woolpack and continued to do so until 1808. The inference must be that Mills was the owner of the inn and that initially Kaye was the tenant; by 1813 the Ramsden rentals show Kaye paying the rent. In 1823 in partnership with James Mills, in a deed which described them both as common brewers, Kaye took the remainder of a lease of land at Quay Street. This was the site of the Quay Street brewery which is first noted in the Huddersfield directory of 1818 being conducted by James Mills & Co. The firm were also maltsters and a rental is recorded in the Ramsden books of 1821/3 under James Mill with the description 'malt kiln'.

Throughout his life descriptions of Kaye in deeds vary according to the nature of the transaction being recorded. In 1813 he is noted as an innkeeper, from 1823 when dealing with brewery or public house properties he appeared as a common brewer. He is first described as a builder in a deed of 1823, but as early as 1808 he was recorded as a mason, a term almost certainly used in the sense of builder. In 1817 when the Leeds Mercury carried an advertisement for the letting of "the building, finishing and finding materials for a methodist chapel in Queen Street, Huddersfield" it was addressed not to builders but to "Masons, carpenters, joiners, plasterers, plumbers and glaziers." In deeds relating to his mills he was a mill proprietor.

Directories show Kaye at the Woolpack in 1822, but by 1828 the licence was held by his brother John who continued to be noted there as innkeeper and publican to 1845, at about which date he appears to have retired. He is noted applying to the Ramsden estate for a lease on three houses at New North Road in December 1844, and it was there that he died in 1851 at the age of 73.

When Joseph Kaye left the Woolpack he did not move far for directories of 1830 to 1845 record him at New Street, variously described as architect, lime burner and merchant, brewer, quarry owner and builder. In later directories he is noted at Buxton Road, no doubt in a house of his own building for he applied to the Ramsden estate in April 1843 for a lease on a house and garden at Buxton Road which had been built one year. He continued to live there until his death in 1858.

• • •

The brewery business was clearly expanded over the years, and it might seem that Kaye held out greater hopes for that facet of his undertakings, along with his mills, than for the building and stone dealing trades, for in his last will of July 1857 he authorised his trustees to wind up the latter and specifically desired that his grandson, when 21, should be placed in the brewery. His reasons, unfortunately, do not appear, but in a will made

ST. PATRICK'S CHURCH

ST. PAUL'S CHURCH

thirteen years earlier he had similarly instructed that his building and stone dealing operations be wound up. In relation to the stipulation in the 1844 will it could have been that he correctly saw that the church building boom was ended, but did not forsee the building boom which was to follow very shortly as the Ramsdens actively encouraged the commercial development of the town. However, the same reasoning could not have prevailed in 1857, and it seems more likely that he realised from long and hard experience that the class of men employed in building and quarrying required a level and standard of supervision which he could not expect to be given by his executors. The Huddersfield Chronicle in his obituary[10] noted;

> He adopted and continued the practice of looking after his business himself. Up to within a very few years of his end, he was never in bed after five in the morning - if at all able to crawl out; but rough or smooth, wet or dry, he was at the main building-work then in hand before six, to see the men on the ground and started on their daily advocation; and then he off to others, quarries or what not, to see that all was going on right there.

So it was that his executors conducted the brewing business to 1855 and continued to own public houses and beer houses in connection therewith. It is difficult to establish at what date the various inns were acquired or came into being, as most were on land of the Ramsden estate, the deeds for which were not registered to the same extent as is found with those for freehold property.

We have seen that Kaye had definitely been involved with the Quay Street brewery from 1823, probably from 1818 as one of the unnamed partners in James Mills & Co., and possibly from an even earlier date. His executors offered the concern for sale by auction in 1885 when it was described as 'Huddersfield old brewery', an old established steam brewery which had been worked for upwards of fifty years. It failed to sell at auction and appears immediately to have been closed and the site developed for housing which was subsequently sold in 1888 together with the coopers shop. In 1880 the executors of Thomas Firth of Toothill had a report prepared[11] on various properties then held by Kaye's executors which clearly indicates why the brewing interests did not sell, "The brewery would not sell well unless a number of tied houses could be sold with it. The plant is old fashioned, the rooms low and inconvenient, the buildings put together like a patchwork." That state of affairs should not be taken as evidence of mismanagement by the executors, the wording of Kaye's will had been legally interpreted as prohibiting the employment within the concern of more capital than was invested at the time of his death.

It has already been noted that Kaye was connected with the Woolpack from as early as 1803, and that it was managed by him or his brother for the next forty years. It was clearly the 'flagship' of the group of outlets, a fact confirmed by the price of £10,400 which it realised when it was finally sold in 1896. The next two in importance seem to have been the Bull & Mouth Inn, fronting Victoria Street and Bull & Mouth Street, and the West Riding Hotel in the block of property on John Street, between Buxton Road and Albion Street. The former was sold for £3,900 in 1885, the latter was not offered until 1888 when, with the shops and warehouses adjoining, it realised £4,075. All the foregoing were purchased by their respective tenants. Lesser houses were the Victoria Inn, Victoria Street, and the George & Dragon Inn on Manchester Street, both of which were auctioned in 1885. The Jacob's Well at Honley was the only freehold property and had been purchased by Kaye in partnership with Joseph Mills in 1841; it too was sold in 1885 when the purchaser was Joseph Harrison, a brewer at Fenay Bridge.

All the outlets previously mentioned had full licences as opposed to the following which were not licensed to sell spirits and were in consequence known as beer-houses. These were all sold in 1885 and were the Unicorn Inn in Victoria Street, the Mechanic's Arms in Castlegate and Rosemary Lane, and the Commercial at Folly Hall which latter was sold to Joseph Lumb & Sons, cotton spinners. With the exception of the Jacob's Well and the Woolpack it is not unlikely that the inns were built by Kaye, probably financed by the profits from his building activities, as useful outlets for the brewery.

It is interesting to examine the population figures of Huddersfield for the first half of the nineteenth century[12], the period when Kaye flourished: -

1801	7,268	1831	19,035
1811	9,671	1841	25,018
1821	13,284	1851	30,876

They disclose an increase of over 300% during the 50 years that Kaye was in business in the town. Related to his principal activities of building and brewing, it is difficult to see how, when once established, he could have failed to prosper with such an increasing population. He did not of course have the field to himself, the main brewers in the area were Bentley & Shaw of Lockwood who also flourished. In building two of his major competitors were John Radcliffe & Co., and the Heywood family, both of whom are noted in the unsuccessful tenders for the erection of the Infirmary in 1829. The former are said to have been founded in 1802 and continue as substantial contractors at the present time. Local buildings for which they are noted include the old Market Hall, Storthes Hall hospital, Cambridge Road Baths and the old Midland Bank premises in Cloth Hall Street. The Heywoods are noted in the Huddersfield Directory of 1818 with John and Joseph of Manchester Street and Granby Street respectively, stone masons. George who tendered for the infirmary was probably of the firm of George & William Heywood who were to build All Saints Church, Netherthong in 1828.

In fact Kaye and John and Joseph Heywood were at one time partners under the style of Joseph Kaye & Co. In 1810 they built the Brown Cow Inn in the Market Place, Huddersfield, for Daniel Armitage[13]. The Brown Cow was an ancient inn, one of the galleried structures which had been built on the east side of the Market Place almost exactly 100 years earlier, and which in 1810 was replaced with an ashlar building at a cost of almost £350.

• • •

No details have been found of any major buildings by Kaye between Thornton Lodge, c.1802, and 1817. There is no doubt, however, that he was engaged on the general development of the town, building offices and shops for an expanding trading centre, and warehouses and mills for a similarly expanding manufacturing and distribution centre. The late John Betjeman credited Kaye with the laying out of the town with wide streets; mistakenly, for there was no way in which he could have been responsible. He was building for clients, hard-headed businessmen whose goal was profit and who would have little regard for the niceties of planning. Effective control lay with, and clearly came from, the Ramsden estate who, owning the land, were able to impose building regulations within the town. Kaye in evidence to the Royal Commission (Appendix B) confirmed this "All the town here belongs to one landlord, Sir John Ramsden, who compels the formation of wide streets, and the building of good straight houses."

That control had not always been exercised in the town is evident from the account given in White's Directory of the West Riding, 1837:-

> It was not till a few years ago that they (The Improvement Commissioners) began to round the corners and widen the contracted parts of the public streets, Dangerous Corner, the ugly obstacle in the passage through the town from Leeds to Manchester vanished in the early part of 1837, by the demolition of the projecting building; behind the site of which a handsome erection, with a fine curved front now presents itself to view. This is only the commencement of a series of projected improvements, among which are, the partial removal of the Horse Shoe Inn, the Boy and Barrel, the Fleece Inn and the Rose and Crown, all of which contract the public avenues, consequently, the removal of their projecting parts, and the substitution of modern fronts, would not only beautify the town, but make the thoroughfares which have so long been a reproach on the inhabitants, as commodious as those of most other towns in the kingdom. The modern streets are

generally spacious and handsome, especially New Street, Buxton Road, King Street and Westgate. At the head of the latter several houses have been removed to widen the approach, and to make room for a cattle market. The Market Place is a large area lined with good houses and shops, mostly rebuilt during the last 50 years.

Is it significant that all the projecting properties were inns? Having said that there had not always been control exercised it is interesting to note an entry in the disbursements of the Ramsden's local agent[14] in December 1768 "Pd for taking down the new building erected in the street by Joshua Mitchell." In view of what has gone before it is hardly surprising to find that Joshua Mitchell was an innkeeper, being listed in the ale house recognisances[15] for the town in 1771.

The minute book of the Commissioners for Lighting, Watching etc. the Town of Huddersfield[16], records in February 1822 "Mr. Kaye be requested to measure a radius of 1,200 yards in the Township of Huddersfield from the place where the Market Cross formerly stood." Such measurement was necessary to ensure that the Commissioners acted only within the area for which they were so authorised. A year later Kaye attended his first meeting in the capacity of a Commissioner.

• • •

Having established that conditions were propitious for business success, the one area in which Kaye could have faced financial danger was the failure of clients for whom he had commenced or completed contracts. That this did happen is shown by his appointment on several occasions as one of the assignees of the estate and effects of insolvent or bankrupt debtors. The first instance noted was in 1808 in respect of Edward Wilcock, a carpenter; Kaye's involvement could have been related to monies loaned to a fellow tradesman or to an outstanding debt on a building contract. In support of the latter theory Wilcock had taken a lease on land at Dam Close, Aspley in 1799, a condition of which was that he was to erect a dwelling house on part of it[17]. By 1808 the site included not only a house but saw-pits and a counting-house.

In June 1832 Kaye was appointed in the matter of Thomas Lockwood of Huddersfield, woolstapler, trading as George Lockwood & Co., the other assignees being Thomas Hannah of Huddersfield and Miles Netherwood of Deighton, both woolstaplers. The assignees were generally the major creditors, and the reason for Kayes involvement may well have been that he had built various properties for Lockwood. An advertisement in the Leeds Mercury of 28th July 1832 gave notice of the sale by auction of valuable leasehold estates in Huddersfield by order of the assignees of Thomas Lockwood, a bankrupt. Several of the lots were in New Street and Buxton Road and included a newly erected dwelling house, two newly erected stables and several newly erected cottages. Kaye was appointed again in 1843 in the case of James Senior of Lascelles Hall and Waterloo, manufacturer of fancy cloths and common brewer.

• • •

On 19th December 1816 the foundation stone of Holy Trinity Church, Huddersfield, was laid; the beginning of a major ecclesiastical contract for Kaye, and the first of a dozen churches or chapels which he was to build in the next fifteen years. Holy Trinity was built wholly at the expense of Benjamin Haigh Allen of Greenhead, who had to promote an enabling Act of Parliament; an undertaking all the more remarkable when one considers that he was at the time only twenty-three years old! It is an illustration of the range of building work which Kaye undertook that having erected the church he can subsequently be found forming burial vaults, providing tombstones and engraving the same at a penny a letter[18].

At about the same time Kaye received another large commission, the building of Queen Street Wesleyan Methodist Chapel. The edifice when completed was the largest methodist chapel in the kingdom, with seating for 2,400 people. Projects of that size called for a contractor of some substance for stone would have to be bought and transported and building work undertaken in advance of contract payments. Banking was well developed in the town by that time, but loans would have to be covered by securities or a first class business standing. As will be seen when considering the Infirmary contracts, principals covered themselves against default by the contractor, for whatever reason, by requiring them to take out bonds. When advertisements were placed inviting tenders for the erection of churches promoted by the Commissioners for Building New Churches, it was a condition that tenders be accompanied by details of two sureties, each in double the amount of the contract.

The public row which followed the placing of the contract for the erection of the Queen Street Chapel throws further light on procedures. On 31st January 1818 a letter was placed in the Leeds Mercury (there being no Huddersfield paper at that time) by Joseph & John Heywood of Huddersfield whose tender for the contract for the new chapel had been unsuccessful despite being £500 less than the successful tender. Subsequent correspondence showed that an even lower tender had not even been considered because Abraham Boothroyd, George Johnson & Co., who submitted it were considered "not sufficient" for the undertaking; the committee were doubtful that they had the substance to complete the contract. That the same doubt did not extend to the Heywoods indicates that they must have been of satisfactory standing and experience. The name of the successful contractor is not disclosed in the correspondence, but Kaye's obituary in the Huddersfield Examiner credited him with the project. The following estimates were given in support of Messrs Heywoods argument; -

The successful one	about £2,000
John & Joseph Heywood	£1,689
Abraham Boothroyd, George Johnson & Co.	£1,558

The allegation made, and not refuted, was that the successful contractor had agreed to do it at the Heywoods calculation, though the fact was disguised by additional payments in respect of vaults which had not been in the original specification, and the possibility that he would 'refund' £100 by way of subscription.

• • •

The minutes of the Huddersfield & Upper Agbrigg Infirmary[19] are informative on the procedures followed in commissioning a public building. There had been pressure for a number of years for the erection of a hospital to serve the town and surrounding area and obviate the necessity of sending patients to Leeds. As early as 1822 Baines Directory noted that Dr. Walker, a physician in the town, recommended the establishment of a House of Recovery in Huddersfield. The need for such a hospital was brought home very forcibly in 1825 on the occasion of a fatal accident during the erection of Ramsden Street Chapel, when the Leeds Mercury reported "The want of an hospital to receive the injured survivors was felt very severely on this occasion, and it is high time this want should be supplied." They renewed the appeal the following week "Confident hopes are entertained that this melancholy catastrophe will lead to the establishment of wards in the Dispensary for the reception of accident patients, a measure which was very warmly and ably advocated last week at the public meeting by Dr. Walker, the Senior physician." The Dispensary was one of the forerunners of the hospital, established in the town ten years, but treating only outpatients.

It may have been the accident which prompted Kaye's election to the committee of the Dispensary in June 1827, a year before the passing of a resolution at the General meeting to the effect that the existing premises were inadequate, that it was time an infirmary was erected and that a sub-committee be formed for the purpose. January 1829 saw the drafting of an advertisement for insertion in the Leeds Mercury inviting designs and specifications for the new building. It is unlikely that Kaye was one of the thirteen architects who submitted twenty plans.

A design by John Oates was accepted and early in May he was able to present details of the various tenders which he had obtained. Those successful were:

Joseph Kaye	Huddersfield	Mason	2,175. 0. 0
John Hepworth & Son	Brighouse	Joiner & Carpenter	1,068. 0. 0
John Newhouse	Huddersfield	Plumber	415. 0. 0
Thomas Clayton	Huddersfield	Plasterer	195. 0. 0
John Crabtree	Halifax	Slater	119.19.11
Joseph Lockwood	Huddersfield	Smith	33. 1. 6
Joseph Lucas	Huddersfield	Painter	35. 0. 0
			4,041. 1. 5

Kaye's tender had been the lowest of the five submitted in respect of mason's work. The five were:

George Heywood	Huddersfield	2,530. 0. 0
John Addey & Co.	Huddersfield	2,546. 0. 0
John Radcliffe & Co.	Huddersfield	2,499. 0. 0
James Nelson & Sons	Bradford	2,486.10. 0
Joseph Kaye	Huddersfield	2,175. 0. 0

As noted Oates's successful plan had been one of twenty and the competition had attracted entries from architects from a wide area. The plans which were placed second and third were from Messrs Hayley & Brown and Messrs Lane, both of which firms were in practice in Manchester. Oates himself had a Manchester connection having submitted a design to the Liverpool Academy in 1813 from a Manchester address, but he was a native of Salterhebble,[20] where his father was a quarry-master. Oates is first noted in practice in Halifax in 1822 and it seems probable that he had been training with a Manchester firm in 1813 when he would have been nineteen years old. He and Kaye had already worked together on the erection of four churches and it could well have been that the two were friends. No doubt Kaye would appreciate an architect with a background of stone-quarrying; at least until the latter's knowledge caught him out! Oates had moved to Huddersfield at about that time, probably because of the volume of work he was undertaking in the area, and he died in the town in May 1831 whilst the Infirmary contract was still going forward.

The successful contractors and their sureties were required to enter into bonds which were prepared by Mr Laycock, solicitor to the Infirmary, and the works were put in hand. A payment was made to Kaye in September 1829 on account of work to date, several further payments followed until a final sum in October 1831 brought his total to £3,499. Probably the bulk of the considerable excess over the contract figure of £2,175 related to the stables, wash-houses and other outbuildings which he had been additionally directed to build in October 1830. As in most contracts there were variations to the specification during building, and a change from 'common wallstone' to 'best hammered dressed stone' is minuted at an extra charge of £65. Whatever the reasons for additional costs it is clear that the whole project was closely monitored by the architect, as appears from the following letter:

Springwood, March 16, 1830

I beg to inform you that I will attend the meeting of the committee of the Huddersfield & Upper Agbrigg Infirmary on the evening of Thursday next the 18th inst. when I hope the committee will take into consideration the circumstances of the Longwood Edge stone introduced by Mr. Joseph Kaye contrary to his agreement instead of the Radcliffe Delph stone and decide whether the same shall be permitted to remain or must be taken down.

I am Sir Yours very respectfully

John Oates

To J.C. Laycock Esq.

It must have been with a certain amount of foreboding that he raised the matter for not only was Kaye a committee member, but by the very scale of his operations at that time he must have stood high in the ranks of the town's leading businessmen. The subsequent resolution, which must have been gratifying to Oates, and which reflects well on the committee, was"That Mr. Oates, the architect, and, under his direction, the Clerk of Works, are hereby instructed to see the terms of the contract and the specifications strictly observed." That the committee was in no way overawed by Kaye appears from a resolution passed at a meeting in August 1831 "That Mr. Joseph Kaye be ordered to clear away the ground of the infirmary ...... within six days." Kaye was present at the meeting and one may perhaps imagine the import of muttered comments on the foregoing which prompted the committee after dealing with other matters, to make the additional resolution "Also that if Mr. Kaye neglect, the committee will do it themselves and charge him the expenses!"

Reverting to a consideration of the masons' tenders noted earlier it will be seen that the four unsuccessful ones all fell within a range of £60; Kaye's however was £300 pounds less than the next lowest, a difference of over 12.5%. It is interesting to speculate on the reasons for such competitiveness; the sheer scale of his operations (he had five churches building) must have given him some advantage in labour utilisation, and his competitors may have had to recruit from his workforce at a premium. He also had control of his own supply of stone which would have been a very material advantage, even without the deceit which he tried to practice in substituting a presumably inferior stone from quarries much closer to the building site. On the other hand the tender may have been pitched low deliberately, even to the extent of foregoing a profit, with the object of securing the contract at all cost, either for purposes of prestige or merely to ensure that it did not go to his competitors. If his motives were for prestige then he must surely have been well satisfied. On 29th June 1831 he had a prominent place in the two mile long procession which preceeded the official opening, before a crowd of 30,000 to 40,000 people.

• • •

We have noted that the specification of the Infirmary called for part of the building to be of Radcliffe Delph stone. That stone was quarried at Sowood in Stainland and was noted for its size and quality. That Kaye was aware of the desirability of having his own quarry for such stone is evidenced by his purchase, as early as 1823, of two acres of land in Stainland[21]. Clearly massive blocks would be necessary for such decorative features as the columns found in both the infirmary and the railway station, and probably the sale of such stone to other builders would be a lucrative proposition. An instance of the use of stone from Kaye's Stainland quarry is to be found in the letters of George Crowther[22], land agent, who records that as a young man in 1831 he had ashlar carted from there for the facing of the family home he was building at Wood in Fixby, a dwelling which still stands. Correspondence relating to the building of the George Hotel reveals that Sowood stone was utilised for the east front of the building. Kaye sold the Stainland land to a farmer in 1854, presumably having been worked out and the site filled and levelled[23].

The control of ones own quarry or quarries must have been of great importance to a substantial builder both in terms of guaranteeing supplies and in providing an advantage in quoting for work. Correspondence relating to quotations for the new George Hotel in 1849 noted "Mr. Kaye can afford to do the masons work cheaper than any of the others as he has the quarries from which the stone will be had." Another letter hopes that "Mr. Kaye will have been able to get out of his two quarries stone large enough for the cornice and blocking." Talking of a proposed covered market place for the town it was observed that Mr. Kaye should reduce his quotation because of the saving on carting from using stone from the Marsh quarry and from the saving on tolls by being allowed to use Greenhead Lane. The latter is an indication of the important item which the cost of cartage and tolls could become in a major contract; imagine how many cart loads of stone would be required for the railway station or the church at Bay Hall!

In the reminiscences mentioned earlier Sir A.K. Rollit recalled driving with his grandfather to his quarries at Sowood, Marsh and Crosland. Kaye had been commissioned to build St. John's Church at Bay Hall by the trustees of Sir J.W. Ramsden deceased, and he approached the local agent of the estate to open a quarry at Cowcliffe on their land; permission was refused as there were already two quarries being worked in that area, by Henry Crossland and George Rhodes, from whom he could purchase wallstones. Henry Crossland was the father of William Henry Crossland who was to become one of the countries foremost architects designing such masterpieces as the Royal Holloway College and Rochdale Town Hall.

Kaye, no doubt wishing for control of his own sources, and probably with a view to maximising profits, then applied to operate a quarry at Marsh Wood on the left hand side of the road to Gledholt from which, many years previously, quantities of stone were used in the construction of Sir John Ramsden's Canal, and which may have been the same quarry which supplied the stone for the first Highfield Chapel in 1771. Kaye received permission in July 1851 and two months later the Ramsden's local agent was enthusing "opening of Marsh quarry a capital thing both for Mr. Kaye and the church ...... may prove a source of revenue, admirable paving stone can be supplied." Kaye had operated a quarry at Marsh at an earlier date, being noted in 1843[24] occupying a stone quarry and thirteen acres of land there. That was not a part of the Ramsden estate, it belonged to William Walker Battye, grandson of a prosperous Huddersfield butcher. Presumably that quarry had been worked out by the time Kaye applied for the Ramsden quarry, or had been taken in hand by the owner. It was possibly Kaye's interests in quarries in the area which led him to become a member of the Marsh Society for the Prosecution of Felons, a body which had been formed at the Woolpack c.1816[25].

Nothing is known of Kaye's quarries at Crosland Moor which his grandson mentioned in his recollections. Kaye was shown in the Register of Electors for the West Riding for 1835 qualifying by right of a farm at Crosland Hill at £50 rent. The following extract from Geology of the Country around Huddersfield & Halifax, 1930, indicates the importance of the area for the supply of stone: -

> The extensive plateau of Crosland Moor to the west of Huddersfield consists of rough rock and here and there is a large number of important quarries which still form one of the main centres of stone quarrying in West Yorkshire.
>
> The town of Huddersfield together with the adjoining villages are very largely built of Crosland Hill stone and there is also a considerable export of the stone to more distant centres.
>
> The majority of public buildings in Huddersfield are built of the material, which appears to weather well and to be admirably adapted to the district. The exception is in the case

of Huddersfield Parish Church where it appears to have weathered badly, but this is due to the frequent error of laying the stone oblique to the bedding planes.

The reference to the Parish Church alludes in much more moderate terms to the building fault which caused the writer of Kaye's obituary to describe it as "the rickety and scabbed-looking thing." The letter reproduced as Appendix A bears on the same subject, and when the writer, the local agent of the Ramsden estate, notes "I have conversed with Mr. Kaye freely on all these matters" we may assume that the technical matters were culled from Kaye.

It really was most unfortunate that the contract for the masons work on the rebuilding of the Parish Church in 1836 did not go to Kaye, or at least to someone with a better understanding of the local stone than was displayed by the builder employed. Kaye had undertaken day-to-day repairs to the church fabric from 1818 and in 1822 had renewed the wall at the south side of the churchyard at a cost of £192.2.11[26]. The contract for the rebuilding went to W. Exley of York who is reported to have submitted a very low estimate and used as much of the material from the old church as he possibly could. Whilst the masonry is known to have been wrongly laid, as much or more blame must be laid to the supervisors of the work as to the builder. The architect was James Pigott Pritchett of York, about whom the Hon. Isabella Ramsden was to write "We must stear clear of Mr. Pritchett, in his profession as an architect he has given the Ramsden family a lesson not to be forgotten (in the works he performed at Brotherton Church) of the instability of his building."

• • •

Apart from stone the builders main raw material was mortar, the principal constituents of which are sand, lime and water. James Bottomley had operated a lime kiln in Huddersfield from 1810 at which date he is noted in the town's rate book paying for land and lime kilns. It is probable that he succeeded William Bottomley who was supplying Joseph Firth with lime in 1802. The earliest reference which has been noted to lime-burning in the town is in 1791 when John Bradley's will[27] mentioned three lime kilns at Lane in the occupation of himself and Henry Sheard. By 1808 other kilns were being operated by Richard Clay at Aspley.

In his will[28] of 1821 James Bottomley appointed Joseph Kaye and William North, a gardener, his executors and guardians of his children. He specifically authorised them to continue his trade of limeburner with the use of all necessary boats and implements. His son Joseph was to be allowed a salary and the profits were to go to the maintenance of his other children; the arrangement to terminate when his youngest daughter attained the age of eighteen and the business, with the exception of the boats, to pass to his said son. These lime kilns were no doubt the same ones which John Bradley had operated, they were situate on the Leeds road adjoining the gas works and the canal, and continued to operate down to the 1850's.

Kaye did not waste the experience which he must have gained in conducting the lime-burning business for Bottomley's children. By 1836 he was renting and working lime kilns at Aspley which had previously belonged to Bradley Clay, the same kilns which in 1808 had been in the occupation of Richard Clay. Kaye continued to operate as a lime burner and merchant for the next twenty years, and it was one of the businesses which he authorised his executors to continue. In the nine months following his death the business showed a profit of £141, but probably the profits, and the benefits of a secure supply, were greater when his building activities were at a peak. Internal plaster also used lime and he would have had excellent outlets to subcontractors and trade connections.

Lime is obtained by burning chalk or limestone in kilns at high temperatures, taking up to 4.5cwt of coal per ton of lime produced, and it would be no accident that the site of the kilns adjoined the canal whence the bulky raw materials could most conveniently and cheaply be brought in. When in 1832 Kaye had been delegated by the infirmary committee to obtain a boat-load of coals they had come from Bradley Clay, and it is likely that the premises at Aspley incorporated coal wharves. Indeed Clay was described as a wharfinger in the list of shareholders of the Huddersfield Banking Co. in 1827 and had, in 1825, been one of the founding directors of theHuddersfield Shipping Co.

It is perhaps a little surprising that Kaye does not appear to have secured his own supplies of coal. Certainly he would have been a major user of coal at his Folly Hall factories and his 'steam' brewery as well as at the lime kilns. Apart from consumption in his various enterprises Kaye may have traded in coal for there is a note relating to Whitacre's mill in 1847 recording that payments had been made to Kaye & Son for cannel coal. There were quite a number of coal pits in the area, Bottomley, the lime-burner had rented one from Joseph Firth as early as 1804, and it may be significant that the father of John Bradley, the above mentioned lime kiln operator, leased collieries from the Ramsden estate.

• • •

We have seen that the quantities of stone used in Kaye's major buildings were huge and the transport side would be almost a business in itself. The stone from his quarries would have to be taken to sites by cart, and as it appears to have been his policy to avoid middlemen, we may assume that he had his own fleet of carts and horses. Some support for this assumption may be drawn from the statement of Native in a series of articles on Huddersfield 70 years ago, which appeared in the Huddersfield Examiner in May 1878. He wrote that "the Riding School became a theatre and then, for a number of years a waggon warehouse." The Riding School had been erected by Kaye in Albion Street c.1818 appearing in the Ramsden rental for the first time in 1818-20 under his name. Whilst it was built, nominally at least, as a facility for the local volunteer yeomanry, it seems possible that Kaye viewed it from the first as a secure compound for his carts and waggons. Haulage of course would be by horse and it is no surprise to learn from the recollections of his grandson that Kaye was a good horseman. This seems very often to have been a natural consequence of a working relationship with horses and was paralleled some years later by the forebears of the present Lord Hanson. Sir A.K. Rollit recalled that for many years before the telegraph came to the town Kaye brought the first news to Huddersfield from Doncaster of the winner of the St. Leger, which was acclaimed by large crowds in Back Green.

Yet another facet of Kaye's string of enterprises, though one for which little evidence appears, was that of coach proprietor. It is probable that he saw it as complementary to his haulage activities, utilising similar resources. In June 1837 Kaye was bound over to keep the peace towards Edward Aspinall, the driver and proprietor of the Accommodation coach[29], the reason is not known, but it may well have related to fierce rivalry which existed between opposition coaches plying the same routes.

• • •

In considering the origin of the infirmary mention was made of the accident during the building of the Ramsden Street Independent Chapel. The building was designed by Messrs Watson & Pritchett of York, the first of a number of local buildings for which J.P. Pritchett senior was to be responsible in the next thirty years.

Kaye was awarded the contract for the masonry and excavation work at a price of £2,819.10.10[30]. The foundation stone was laid on 14th July 1824 and Kaye's section of the work must have been well advanced when, on 26th April 1825, there befell a disastrous accident at the site. The tragedy was occasioned by the breaking of a bearer which supported a platform 50 foot above ground on which at the time were sixteen people[31]. Three of the men died the same day and within a week a fourth died of injuries received. The town was shocked by the accident and an immediate subscription was opened for the relief of the dependents, twenty-two children having been left fatherless. Within two weeks the fund stood in excess of £400, a not inconsiderable sum. The other immediate outcome of the accident was, as we have seen, a renewed call for an infirmary in the town.

• • •

Building and quarrying are by their very nature dangerous trades and even without Kaye's testimony, quoted in his obituary, "I have never been laid up for a single day by sickness not occasioned by accident." we may have supposed that during a working life of over 50 years in those trades he would not have escaped without accident.

Perhaps because of the risks they faced daily masons were a hard working hard living breed. Where records exist of building operations it is usual to find allowances to the masons for beer, probably an old established tradition. Bruce in Highfield Chapel Centenary notes "gifts of ale with which masons and labourers were stimulated to increase their diligence and hasten the execution of their work." An ingenious justification, no doubt tongue in cheek, for a perquisite which had accrued to the trade over the centuries and that could not be withdrawn without incurring the wrath of a volatile body of men. In correspondence relating to the erection of the new George Hotel it was stated that it was usual to give the masons and labourers a supper once all the foundations were dug and the laying of the footings commenced. The Ramsden correspondence contains a letter to the local agent requesting an explanation of the 'Flooring' and 'Footing pots' mentioned in connection with the new George Hotel; his reply unfortunately does not appear, but they were probably payments for beer at differing stages of progress.

The masons appear to have been a militant body quick to take advantage of any circumstances which strengthened their bargaining power. The Leeds Mercury in 1834 reported on the 'turn-out' of the Manchester stone masons "This body which has ever been foremost in the strikes of the building trade is again out. They were out last year." In the early months of 1848 it was noted in connection with the erection of new offices at Longley Hall that the workmen had struck and there was a demand for an increase of sixpence a day for labour. However, by November that year an architect was writing that "the masons in Huddersfield are at this time almost unoccupied." In 1852 Kaye was under pressure to effect a speedy completion of the new church at Bay Hall but feared a turn out of his men who were employed in hewing and dressing stone if they learned that it had to be finished in so short a time. It was suggested that a batch of men could be obtained from Manchester, Liverpool or Glasgow if necessary, and particularly noted that masons from Scotland would be preferred to southerners from having

JOSEPH KAYE
Artist and date unknown

JOSEPH KAYE
by Joseph Howell 1852

worked with hard kinds of stone.

Kaye was particularly worried about a strike at that time for the simple reason that the building trades in Huddersfield had never been so busy. He complained that he was compelled to pay good wages to indifferent hands, paying some four shillings a day who did not earn him two shillings. The daily rate may be compared with the two shillings a day which was paid to masons in 1771 when Highfield Chapel was being erected. Of five masons from York who were set on by Kaye three worked only one day as they found the stone too hard for them.

No reference has been seen to the employment of Irishmen in Kaye's building or quarrying operations though there is little doubt that a good number would be employed over the years as labourers. The great majority of immigrant Irish seldom had skills to suit them to occupations other than labouring, though subsequent generations probably progressed to become skilled stone masons. That Kaye built the Roman Catholic church of St. Patrick in Huddersfield may have been due purely to commercial factors, but it could have indicated a relationship with the Irish community. That there was such a relationship is probable from the fact that a room in the Woolpack yard was used on Sundays for several years prior to the opening of the church, in 1832, for the purposes of Holy Mass[32]. What more natural than that the Irish community should approach the most prominent person and property owner with whom they had contact, as employees, to assist them in the provision of temporary accommodation for their worship, and when the time came, to erect their new church.

It has been suggested that Kaye designed St. Patrick's Church. The church and its associated buildings are arguably the most handsome ecclesiastical buildings in the town and there is no evidence that Kaye's undoubted capabilities ran to architectural design of such a high order. In fact the designer was an established Leeds architect, who designed both St. Anne's and St. Patrick's Roman Catholic churches in Leeds, as appears from a report in the Leeds Mercury of 1st September 1832. "The new Catholic chapel at Huddersfield is to be opened on 26th of this month. A beautiful gothic structure built entirely of a fine white stone and reflects great credit on the architect, Mr. Child of Leeds, and the builder, Mr. Kaye of Huddersfield." The church was recently cleaned and, if one can overlook the present entrances, a later addition, must present almost the aspect which it had when newly opened. One may imagine what a pleasant vista New North Road bore in its early days, flanked on one side by the Infirmary in classical style and on the other the gothic St. Patricks.

• • •

Kaye was repeatedly classified in directories from 1822 to 1857 as, among other headings, an architect. It is likely that the whole of his architectural output was of a utilitarian nature. No evidence has been seen of his designing public buildings or any building of architectural interest. John Betjeman in an article unworthy of his popular talent, in the Weekend Telegraph in October 1964, credited Kaye with the design of both the Infirmary and St. Paul's Church. He was completely in error, there has never been any doubt that both were designed by John Oates.

Kaye had great experience of building housing and no doubt prepared what plans were necessary for many of them. Probably he would be responsible for plans of any buildings he erected on his own account: his house in Buxton Road, shops, offices, inns and warehouses in the town and his mills at Folly Hall. From his experience in erecting and running the mills at Folly Hall, the first of which was the largest in the area at the time of its building, it is probable that he was reponsible for many mills in and around Huddersfield. There is evidence that Kaye had at least one very able industrial architect on his staff. The obituary of James Leech[33] in 1870 recorded "he commenced in the capacity of clerk in the offices of the late Joseph Kaye Esq, builder and contractor, continuing to the death of Kaye in 1858. As an architect for the erection of mill property he stood at the head of all his compeers in the district."

Following the destruction by fire of his mill at Woodhouse, John Whitacre advertised for plans for a new mill. It would appear that he offered a prize for the best plan submitted for a handbill was circulated in June 1844[34] detailing various plans which were missing from the counting house at Woodhouse. Among them was "Prize plans and elevation of the proposed new mill by Joseph Kaye." Whitacre did not in fact employ Kaye either as builder or supervising architect, his practice in building was to buy in the materials and let the labour. He had the plans redrawn twice, first by David Hanson and then by Henry Bake, the latter a Manchester architect whose first project it was.

• • •

One of Kaye's major enterprises was that of factory proprietor, with extensive mills at Folly Hall. He first leased land from the Lockwood estate in December 1825[35], in partnership with Thomas Dinsley, a respected land surveyor in the town. The land was part of a close called Little Steps at Folly Hall Bridge: in 1829[36] he was assessed upon a new factory. That mill situate beside the River Colne, was burnt down in 1844 and was replaced by a six storey mill known as the 'old' or '60 horse' mill from the capacity of the steam engine which provided the power. From the report of a further fire on the site in 1856, which will be mentioned later, we learn the following details on the origin of the mill. The original mill was commenced in 1825 but by the end of that year banks were failing and many building projects were stopped, amongst them the large Folly Hall mill, the operations of the builder being suspended some two years. In 1827 work was resumed and the mill, then the largest in the district, proceeded to completion.

The above does not accord with the date when Kaye first took the land. The explanation may be that the mill was originally started for a client, but with the general financial collapse the project was aborted and the interest in the building passed to Kaye who, to make the best of the situation, took a lease on the land and proceeded with the work as sufficient funds became available from his other activities. If this theory is correct his entry into that major sphere of operations was entirely fortuitous. However, the fact that the lease was not completed until after the building had commenced may have been due to a practice commonly adopted later in the century when the engrossing of the lease was left until the building was erected and the exact dimensions of the land could be accurately ascertained. If that procedure was being adopted one would not have expected the lease to be made until 1827 or later. The impending crisis of December 1825 may have caused the proprietors of the Lockwood estate to proceed with all haste.

In 1834 Kaye leased further land adjoining the above on which he erected another six storey mill known as the 'centre' or '40 horse' mill, together with a five storey weaving factory. Over the next ten years, additional land was taken and a warehouse and four storey '25 horse' mill added. In the early days when mills on such a scale were a novelty the site must have been very impressive. G.S. Phillips found it worthy of mention in his Walks Round Huddersfield in 1848. "In my neighbourhood on the Manchester Road, the prospect over the Lockwood valley is very beautiful. At the foot of my garden run the canal and a few yards beyond it the river. Beyond the river lie green fields full of tenters, to the left stand the factories of Joseph Kaye, like so many Aladdin palaces, with their hundreds of windows and tall steeple chimnies." Perhaps at the present time when familiarity and grime make it difficult to appreciate any fairy-tale qualities of our great mills the imagination may be sparked by the magnificent photograph of the Colne Valley at night reproduced in Miss Bentley's Colne Valley Cloth.

The buildings were well known as Kaye's factories and no doubt served as an additional advertisement of his building activities.

Danger of fire was a perennial problem in textile factories; the raw materials were highly combustible and a spark could easily be caused by the machinery.

We have already noted that two of Kaye's factories were destroyed by fire. The fire which ocurred in June 1844 gutted the oldest (number 1) mill, a six storey range, seventeen windows long, despite the efforts of Kaye's own fire engine and those of Armitage Bros. of Milnsbridge, John Brooke & Son of Armitage Bridge and the Leeds & Yorkshire Insurance Co. The latter was disabled when the intake pipe was placed in the reservoir without a rose and the engine filled with dirt. It was a still morning and though the doors and windows of the other six storey mill caught fire with the intense heat the building was saved. The contemporary report in the Leeds Mercury estimated the damage at £40,000 and noted that there was partial insurance of £6,000. Twelve years later on the occasion of the other great fire it was recorded that Kaye's share of the loss was upwards of £25,000 and that the insurance cover on the buildings had been reduced from £8,000 to £4,000 in consequence of an increase in insurance rates.

Kaye was in the habit of raising money on the mills and one would assume that the mortgagors would have insisted on insurance cover sufficient to protect their interest. The comparatively small sums of insurance on both occasions may in fact have been for that purpose. It is possible that Kaye took a conscious decision not to cover the remainder; he would be well aware of the dangers and the consequences, it was only six years earlier that a disastrous fire gutted the extensive uninsured premises of Joshua Lockwood at Manchester Street. One must, however, place serious reservations on the values expressed in the various newspaper reports. The Chronicle in 1856 stated that Mr.Kaye had expended more than £120,000 upon the mills and shafting. However, probate of his will two years later was at 'under £45,000', and a valuation of c.1869 put the mills and associated buildings at approximately £23,000. As the latter was for purposes of partition between disputing beneficiaries it is likely to have been the more realistic figure.

In 1856 there was another fire on the Folly Hall site in which the centre factory was destroyed. The fire was discovered soon after 5am and was immediately tackled by Kaye's own fire engine using water from one of the reservoirs on the site, unfortunately the hose was located too deeply causing the engine to silt-up. It was suggested that if it had been working the damage might have been under £10 instead of over £20,000. For the remainder of the day the town's and the Leeds & Yorkshire Insurance Co's engines fought the blaze until it was contained at 9pm. Kaye himself was unaware of the fire, he had fallen in the house the previous Sunday, after returning from chapel, and broken two ribs. He immediately set about rebuilding; his last project, it was almost complete when he died in March 1858.

Clearly one of the answers to the ever present danger of fire was to have ones own fire engine and trained brigade. A number of the larger mills were so equipped and Kaye's brigade continued to be maintained by his executors to 1872 by which time they were beginning to dispose of the factories. In the advertisement for sale the '60 horse' was given the alternative name of 'fire-proof mill', and it was particularly noted that "the mills are protected by water-plugs on each landing and reservoirs, wells and pipes to convey water from the canal."

In erecting the mills Kaye must have seen an opportunity for an investment in which to employ the profits or cash surpluses of his other activities. It seems clear that he had a natural instinct for business. He avoided direct investment in the textile industry, where fortunes were being made and lost, but obtained a good return on his investment by letting off room and power within the factories to textile manufacturers and allied trades. His only direct involvement appears to have been in the milling or fulling of cloth, probably as a service to his tenants which he had been unable to farm out. In accounts covering the nine months following his death milling was the only activity which lost money (£108). That would not arouse undue concern when set against the profit from the factories of £3,117. The factories which appear to have been valued at about £20,000 at that time but which no doubt cost Kaye a good deal less than that, were thus yielding something in the order of 15%! However, the success of the investment had not been immediately assured, in 1829 it appears that he and Dinsley were struggling to find tenants and a great part of the mill was still unoccupied[37].

The first of the mills to be sold, in 1872, were the '40 horse' and the weaving factory, both of which were sold to Joseph Lumb and Son, existing tenants of part of the premises, who still remain on the site.

• • •

There were at Folly Hall, as might be expected from the size of the operation, various ancillary services. The Ramsden rentals of 1848/50 record Kaye paying rent of £4 in respect of gas works. A number of the larger mills in the area had their own gas works, Kaye's probably supplied the lighting for his factories. It seems likely that Kaye was one of the 'leading inhabitants' who commenced the private gas works at Leeds Road in 1821. In 1828 the commissioners for Lighting and Watching resolved[38] "that Messrs. Brook, Booth & Kaye, for the gas proprietors, agree to light Huddersfield .... for seven years." Brook would be Barnard Henry Brook a gas engineer who in 1829 was assessed for Poor Rate in respect of 'gas works.' Booth was probably the town's leading ironmonger, and it could well be that all three were very much involved in the creation of the actual works. In 1861 the Huddersfield Gas Co. was incorporated by Act of Parliament to provide the town's gas supply. A proportion of the shares were allotted to shareholders of the previous company, which would have been the origin of the Huddersfield Gas Co. shares held by Kaye's executors which were valued c.1869 at £5,800.

Also on the Folly Hall complex was a foundry, first noted in the Ramsden rental in May 1837. It was probably established in connection with the upkeep of the gearing etc. for the mills, but would no doubt serve other facets of Kaye's activities.

In addition to the industrial activities at Folly Hall Kaye held land which was let for agriculture. In a letter[39] to the Court Leet in 1857, complaining of cattle trespass he stated that he had occupied a field at Folly Hall upwards of 50 years, showing that he had had interests in the area long before the factories were established.

• • •

We have already noted the lack of factual detail surrounding Kaye's origins and his early years. His obituary in the Huddersfield Chronicle recorded "Without the advantage in his youth of anything like what is now known by the term 'education', scarcely able to do more than write his name." Probably Kaye had attended some Dame school in the town for a few years, but the lack of formal education appears not to have hindered his progress in the slightest.

It is a pity that Kaye did not have a biographer among his contemporaries, for we are limited to indirect sources in attempting to deduce something of his character. Hordern, the Ramsden's local agent who would have had a good deal of contact with him wrote[40] "Joe Kaye was a funny old man. He has been known to say after taking a contract for a church, that he had forgotten the estimate for the tower, but I never heard of his getting paid extra." Hordern also recorded an episode in connection with the building of the railway station. Half way through the construction the railway company told Kaye they could not proceed to plan because of the expense, he said he would be happy to have the work measured and be paid off but that they would find they would have as much to pay as if he had completed the contract which he had taken at a very low price!

After the last fire at his mills in 1856 the Huddersfield Chronicle in a detailed report wrote of him "At his time of life this is a heavy infliction to bear. It was cheering to see the philosophy with which the venerable old man met the disaster "I had nothing when I begun the world, and I cannot take anything away with me." He was then and during the day undertaking his ordinary business as well as sickness would permit, just as if nothing like a disaster had occurred."

In his old age Kaye became something of a patriarch in the town, as the above report said, a venerable old man. In 1851 a dinner was held at the Woolpack to honour the newly elected Commissioners at which he presided when it was said of him [41]"Few had more to do with the prosperity of Huddersfield than Mr. Kaye. He had been in business above half a century." Two years later he presided at the Annual Meeting and dinner of the Licensed Victuallers and the proposal of his health noted "He had been a landlord, was now a great builder, almost an architect, who had built streets and almost the whole town, to the great advantage of health and the sanitary conditions of the locality." Kaye said he could not make a speech as he was too old! He did however respond following a toast by Bentley Shaw who characterised him as "the Barry of Huddersfield". He recalled that he had known the town when there was only one druggist, a widow woman named Brook, only one barbers shop where there were then 74, when from Brick Buildings down to Chapel Hill and the Cloth Hall were all fields, and when there was not a single long chimney in it. The statement that he was almost an architect confirms what has already been noted on that point.

Kaye's obituary spoke of him in glowing terms, as obituaries do. "One who goes down to the grave full of years and of honour - if honour is ever achieved by eminent success in the walk of life a man is thrown into, or by kindliness of nature, frankness of disposition, joyous social intercommunication, and the highest integrity in the dealings of man with man." We cannot think, however, that he would have received such an eulogy if his neighbours, friends and townsfolk did not in general concur. Perhaps one of the benefits of living to a ripe old age is that events in earlier life which might mar one's character are largely forgotten.

It was forty years since the scandal of the Queen Street Chapel tenders and nearly thirty years since he had practiced his deceit in the building of the Infirmary. In 1836, twenty-two years earlier, he had been convicted under the Factories Act of allowing children under thirteen years of age to work in excess of nine hours a day. These are known character deficiencies, how many more were there which are not now known?

There is no doubt that Kaye ranked alongside the leading tradesmen of the town and he took an appropriate role in public affairs. He was on the committee of the Dispensary, and its successor, the Infirmary. He was a founder commissioner under the Lighting and Watching Act of 1820, and under the 1827 Act for supplying the town with water. He was a trustee of the Act for maintaining the Wakefield to Austerlands Turnpike and is noted chairing the town's Vestry Meeting[42].

UPPER FACADE, METHODIST CHAPEL, QUEEN STREET

BRITANNIA BUILDINGS

He was recorded amongst subscribers for benevolent causes with a donation of £20 in 1854 to the Patriotic Fund, for relief of distress after the Crimean War, and in 1852 with a gift of £50 to the Holmfirth Flood subscription. He was on the committee of the Huddersfield Anti Corn Law Association in 1839 and five years later subscribed £100 to the Free Trade cause.

There are indications in the correspondence of the Ramsden estate of the respect in which Kaye was held by their advisors, and presumably by the family. In 1849 when they wanted advice on the rental to be charged for the buildings and machinery at Newtown woollen mills, their local agent wrote to Kaye and to George Crosland, founder of one of the leading woollen manufacturing concerns in the area. Kaye had replied by the following day with his detailed calculations. In the planning stage of the new George Hotel the architect had been instructed to avail himself of Kaye's advice as to prices "not as a contractor but as a well known tenant and builder of repute, capable of giving a correct judgement." He is known to have worked for Sir John Lister Kaye, having erected a barn at Grange Ash in 1823 at a cost of £163. At the same time he had been engaged to inspect mason's work at Dalton Mill and to quote for the erection of two lodges, in which he was unsuccessful[43].

There is a good deal of correspondence preserved relating to the building of St. John's Church at Bay Hall. The initial impression one has is of great confidence in Kaye to pursue the building with correctness and speed. Within a few months, however, the architect was complaining "I cannot move Kaye, he will not bestir himself to get men ...... he has but one pace and that a very slow one." and again "Mr. Kaye is a wonderfully slow and immoveable person. The tower is rising at the rate of four inches or so a week." It must be remembered of course that Kaye was at that time in his seventies, a point which the estate's local agent noted "I have pressed ... upon him more that is quite pleasant towards an old man whose energies and activity are failing somewhat rapidly of late." Perhaps we should overlook these criticisms in favour of a report of November 1852 which recorded "Mr. Tite (later Sir William Tite, an eminent London architect) was quite delighted with the new church and expressed a high opinion of the masonry and general character and details of the whole building."

One of Kaye's properties in Huddersfield was the Guild Hall. The origins and naming of the property have never been satisfactorily explained. One account suggested it was built towards the end of the eighteenth century for use by merchants with business at the Pack Horse Inn. No reasons were given for the suggestions and there appears to be no logic behind them. The view of Philip Ahier[44], who did so much for local history in the area, that it was erected between 1837 and 1845, appears to be nearer the mark. It is listed in the town rate book in 1843, and meetings are reported to have been held there in 1840 and 1841. The Ramsden rentals indicate that the land was originally the holding of Lockwood but was in the hands of Kaye by 1835. It seems probable from the date that the Lockwood was Thomas, woolstapler, who was made bankrupt in 1832 and for whom Kaye was an assignee. If that was the case it is possible that the building was erected by Lockwood as a wool warehouse. Certainly the large windows of the front elevation indicate a specialist use.

The earliest noted use of the style Guild Hall is in a report of a lecture there in November 1840, and it may have been so designated by Kaye. It seems possible that, recognising a lack of public meeting places in the town he set out to create one, either by building it or by utilising a property he already held. From the 1840's it was used for public meetings including the Free Trade League (which Kaye supported) and the Huddersfield Peace Society. The town's Petty Sessions were held there in the decade to 1857 and the early elections of the town's Improvement Commissioners were conducted there. From 1848 the premises were occupied, free of rent, on the sabbath as a Sunday School by Ramsden Street Chapel, and following Kaye's death the building was sold to the chapel for £525.

• • •

Two portraits of Kaye are known, both now held by Kirklees Art Gallery. The artist and date of the earlier painting are unknown, it is a half length portrait showing Kaye in a blue coat with gilt buttons, waistcoat and knee breeches with one of his factories in the background. Sir A.K. Rollit who presented it in 1897 said it was a good likeness of the subject.

The other picture was commissioned from a local artist, Joseph Howell, in 1852, by friends of Kaye, for presentation to the infirmary. Among those who contributed to the cost were Sir John Ramsden and his agent George Loch, the latter writing that "Mr. Kaye is highly respectable and deserving." The presentation of the three-quarter length portrait, in the background of which are views of the Station and the George Hotel, took place at the Woolpack on Mayday 1852.

The reason why many of the events with which Kaye was connected took place at the Woolpack was not, of course, coincidence; he owned the inn and, if we may read a little into his obituary, was a regular patron. Relating his death the Chronicle noted "On Monday he was stirring in the town as usual; and on the evening of that day was in his accustomed place 'by the ingle nook' where for some 50 years or more he has been nightly to be found." We may be sure that he was not by someone else's ingle nook!

We have made passing references to Kaye's family, and if we know little of his background we have a much better picture of his immediate family.

He was first married on 6th February 1803 at Huddersfield Parish Church to Hannah Rigg, by whom he had had a daughter, Elizabeth, the previous September. A son John was born in December 1804 and another, John William in 1812. None of these children survived to adulthood. The first to survive was Hannah who was born about 1809 and who remained a spinster until December 1844 when she married John Armitage, a Paddock merchant. The second surviving child was Eliza born about 1811 who in 1839 maried John Rollit, the son of a Hull cabinet maker.

Another daughter, Ellen was baptised in June 1814 and eventually married Charles Bradshaw, the son of Kaye's friend, Benjamin Bradshaw the Huddersfield surgeon.

The first surviving son was Joseph junior, or Joe, born about 1816 on whom his father no doubt placed high hopes. As is so often the case the child of a strong man proved to be a weakling, and Joe was to prove a great disappointment to his father. In his first will of 1844 Kaye left a one fifth interest for the benefit of Joe, but he was to have it only in the form of an interest for life, the income being paid to him monthly and he having no power to anticipate or control the funds. Provisions which normally indicate a bankrupt, but in this case possibly just a profligate.

The census of 1851 shows Joseph junior, described as a retired brewer, lodging with Sarah Moseley an unmarried dressmaker of his own age, who had daughters of seven and nine. Joe died two years later and nothing further is known of the Moseleys. The girls may have been Kaye's granddaughters but no evidence appears and no trace has been found of any formal provision being made for them.

The other surviving son was William Henry who was born in January 1819. Like his brother he seems to have opted for a life of retirement, in 1851 he was living with his wife in Quay Street described as 'formerly merchant.' He outlived his father by only four years, dying at Wiesbaden, and had no issue.

Kaye's first wife died in 1836 aged 52, and five years later he married Eliza Aspinall, a widow aged thirty three, some thirty years his junior. If the circumstances suggest a fortune hunter it is not confirmed by the facts. Eliza came from a family of well-to-do woollen merchants, the Days of Moldgreen, and under Kaye's will although she was generously provided for with an annuity of £150, she inherited none of his estate all of which eventually devolved on his six grandchildren. Kaye's true regard for Eliza may be gauged from his instructions that she was to be guardian of his deceased daughter's son.

With two sons who did not appear to have inspired him and who failed to provide family succession Kaye leant increasingly to his daughters' sons. Hannah who predeceased him left only one child, Lewis William Armitage for whom Kaye made special provision in his will leaving him £100 a year to age twenty-one when he desired that he be placed in the brewery. It seems that Lewis William, in accord with Kaye's wish, was brought up by Eliza Kaye with whom he was living in 1861, when still a scholar. He married but appears to have had no issue and it is perhaps significant that his grave in Huddersfield cemetery tells us nothing of him except that he was 'grandson of the late Joseph Kaye, builder etc, of this town."

The sons of Eliza Rollit did not receive any special attention in their grandfather's will as their mother was still living. There was however a close connection, Huddersfield Parish Registers carry a record at 8th October 1841 of the baptism of Albert Kaye the son of John and Eliza Rollit of Hull who had previously been baptised at Hull in June of the same year. There is other evidence of Kaye's interest in this particular grandson. In 1918 there was correspondence[45] as to who was the earliest depositor in the Huddersfield Savings Bank and Sir Albert Rollit, as he then was, noted that his grandfather had made a deposit for him on the occasion of his christening. In the same letter he recalled driving with Joseph Kaye to his various quarries.

Albert Kaye Rollit became a solicitor like his father before him; he was twice Mayor of Hull and received wide public honours including a knighthood. He became a Freeman of Hull and London, and, in 1894, of Huddersfield, in recognition of his services to the free library movement and of assistance which he rendered, as a Member of Parliament, to the passage of local bills. He married for his second wife the widow of the Duke of Sutherland, the richest of all peers, by whom it is said he had £100,000 a year! It is refreshing to find one descendant of Joseph Kaye who succeeded in his own right.

It is fitting that Kaye's tombstone survives in the Parish Churchyard, a substantial monument to Huddersfield's premier builder who still has many undedicated monuments in the town, in the form of the buildings which he raised.

KAYE TOMBSTONE, HUDDERSFIELD PARISH CHURCH

APPENDIX A

Longley Hall
11th August 1851

Sir,

Bayhall Church

Mr. Kaye has been proceeding vigorously with putting in the footings and building the foundation wall of the south side of the church - this portion of the wall is now up to the level of the ground, and they will now proceed with the laying of the footings, and building the foundation wall of the tower and the other side and ends of the church.

I must say that so far as the works have proceeded, Mr. Kaye is doing the work admirably, and in the most substantial manner possible - the stones comprising the footing are of an immense size and thickness, and well bedded and fastened with small stones and plenty of well ground mortar. The large footings are supplied both from Crosland Hill and Marsh quarries - the north wall is now up to the level of the ground and is better than four feet thick, and I should say capable of sustaining any possible weight of wall. The **foundation** stone is now on the ground, and will weigh from 8 to 10 tons as Mr. Kaye informs me - you will have some idea of the size, when I tell you that 8 horses were required to draw it along the new Road to its destination.

A portion of the wall stones from Crosland Hill are on the ground, and a sample of the proposed manner of walling is being set in dry courses for Mr. Butterfields inspection and approval. The specimen of stone appears very good, of a strong hard grit and likely to withstand the weather, and not liable to peel off or perish by long exposure.

But everything in connection with this very important consideration, depend on the manner in which the front wall stones are worked and laid. They should be worked and laid with (to use a local term) **with the teeth outwards,** which is intended to convey the meaning that the stone should be walled as they lie in the quarry - on their bed - for instance, a square block of stone as it lay on its bed, is cut up into divisions - the face where divided is the teeth or interior of the stone. It is very necessary that this course should be followed with the Crosland Hill stone, most of which is apt to perish and **shell off** if the bed be put outwards. In consequence of the main portion of the outer walling being of rough random work it will not be difficult to obtain all the stone of the quality I describe. Care must also be taken that all the ashlar work of the buttresses and coins etc, of the tower should be so worked and walled - of course **one** side of all the **corner** stones must have the **bed** outwards. Mr. Kaye thinks with me, that the Cowcliffe stone will answer very well for the outer walling in rough random courses, either mixing it with the Crosland Hill stones, or using one kind of stone in one side or end of the church, and the other kind of stone in another. The strongest kind of stone with the 'teeth' invariably outwards, should be used in the building of the **south side and west end**.

I have conversed with Mr. Kaye freely on all these matters, and I must say from all that I can observe and have yet seen he appears to be more than usually anxious to do everything in the very best, most durable and approved manner and I do not mention them now to you with the least impression on my mind, that Mr. Kaye will not do the work well and thoroughly substantial, or that he will overlook the full and honest carrying out of the important details I have named, especially in such a building as a church. But I have been anxious that you should be fully aware of all that constitutes the realisation of a perfect and durable structure, such as the church in question will no doubt be. But nevertheless, it may be of service that you should convey to Mr. Butterfield if you think proper, your wishes that he will be good enough to see that the party who may be sent as Clerk of the Works, attends properly to the carrying out of the various essentials in the erection of the outer **walls** to which I have imperfectly alluded. It very often happens that the working masons in spite of very positive instructions from their employer are careless and inattentive, from a desire to save themselves trouble and attention to secure the necessary quality and strength of work.

Agreement with Mr. Kaye - The execution of this was deferred at the request of Mr. Kaye, in consideration of the precise total amount of the estimated cost not having been ascertained, in consequence of the painters work having been put down at so low an estimate as was quite inadequate to secure the proper execution of the work. The estimate of the plasterers work was also somewhat lower than what was considered necessary to secure a good and efficient job. Mr. Kaye has however asked for another estimate of the painting from Burman and Calvert, and after it has been sent in, he will decide on the amount of painters work. I believe he will decide upon North doing the plasterers work at a little more than the lower estimate out of the four former tenders - North is the tradesman who has done the work of the New George Hotel so well.

Mr. Kaye seemed to object when Mr. Fenton read over the Agreement to him, about the time allowed for completing the whole work, namely, the **1st September 1852.** He wishes before signing to have some further conversation with Mr. Butterfield on this point, and also in reference to the total amount of his contract. If the winter be mild, I think he ought to finish on the 1st September 1852 - at all events it may be as well to hold him to that time.

I have omitted to say that the colour of the Cowcliffe stone is almost the same as that of Crosland Hill, of a less strong quality but with a finer and closer grain and it looks exceedingly well when the face is pitched.

It will of course be proper that all instructions and agreements as to the stone etc., should come thro' Mr. Butterfield, and you will readily see that I have written this letter from no possible wish to interfere, but merely from a desire that you should be aware of everything having a tendency to promote the efficiency and general excellence of the structure now so well commenced.

I have the honor to be Sir,
Your most obed faith Servant
Alexr Hathorn

George Loch Esq.
Worsley Old Hall

THORNTON LODGE

APPENDIX B

APPENDIX TO THE FIRST REPORT OF THE COMMISSIONERS OF INQUIRY INTO THE STATE OF LARGE TOWNS AND POPULOUS DISTRICTS

(Royal Commission 1844.)

HUDDERSFIELD. Mr. JOSEPH KAYE, Builder.

How many houses have you built in Huddersfield?
I believe that I have built nearly one-third of Huddersfield.

What number of men do you employ?
I now employ about 250, at other times I have employed about 1,100 men.

Have you observed the mode in which other towns are built and new houses erected?
If there had been a Building Act in Huddersfield it would have been of great advantage to the town; that is if it regulated the drainage; if it regulated the cleansing of the town in respect to the privies. All the town here belongs to one landlord, Sir John Ramsden, who compels the formation of wide streets, and the building of good straight houses. I think it would have been well for other towns to have had regulations as to the width and directions of the streets. I think provision should be made for having areas in front of houses, as it tends to keep them dry.

Are the small houses in Huddersfield built with party walls?
The walls are usually built a brick in length, that is nine inches in thickness.

Have you ever found fires extend through the walls?
No, I never have. A fire took place in the next house to mine this morning; it is a grocer's shop, and a large quantity of paper they had burned very rapidly, and consumed the whole of the things in the shop before it was put out, but the fire did not extend to my house at all. I have heard of fires extending from house to house in other towns but not in this.

Do you conclude that it is not requisite to provide in respect to this town for the building of party walls for protection against fire?
I certainly conclude not; there is no occasion to make the houses more than a brick in length in thickness.

Do you find that fires are very frequent amongst the houses occupied by persons of the labouring classes?
They are very rare indeed.

There appears to be a large proportion of the town where the houses are not properly drained. Suppose it to be provided that they should be drained and cleansed on a principle similar to the water closet, what would be the first obstacle to the accomplishment of that object?
The first obstacle would be the expense.

If the work were done on a large scale, and under regulation, would not the persons having charge of the sewers, or other local public works, be enabled to do it not only better but much cheaper, than private individuals could do it for themselves?
I should think they might do it one-third cheaper, and certainly much better; all the little builders are quite strangers to such work.

If the persons having charge of the public sewers and drainage were enabled to raise the money for doing this by loan, and were to repay the principal and interest for the works by a rate spread over a period of years, would not such an arrangement remove the chief objections in respect to expense to the drainage of old houses?
I certainly think it would be an excellent thing, especially for the houses which are done by working men. It is the practice in this town for working men to put into what is sometimes called a building club; sometimes a money club. When they have accumulated perhaps fifty pounds, they will go and build a house which costs perhaps seventy or eighty, but are unable to complete it. The drainage of these houses is particularly bad. The privies are the last thing erected, and they are generally very badly done. They have no capital to get on farther. In all such cases the plan proposed, which would avoid the necessity of an immediate outlay, would be a great advantage. It would be a capital thing for the labouring classes here to charge for the drainage and cleansing and laying water on in the old houses as a rent. It would be one of the best things that could be done. I believe the inhabitants would like it. I have read the printed note on the principle of defraying such expenses, and I see nothing in it that is against my mind. It would greatly facilitate each street paying for its own sewers, which would be far better when they were paid for as a rent, than charging the expense on a district.

It is stated that in all those houses of the labouring classes where the water is already laid on, that if it were done on a large scale a cheap apparatus of the nature of a water-closet might be laid on, with glazed pot soil pipes to carry off all the refuse and slops from the house, and make it clean, at an expense of £2 or £3 per tenement, involving a rate or additional rent of 2- or 3/- per annum. Do you believe that the labouring classes would after seeing the work done in some instances, so far appreciate the advantages of the additional cleanliness, and making the house 'always sweet', as to be

willing to pay 2/- or 3/- per annum for it?
My idea is that they would. In the areas for good houses we now put water - closets for the servants; they are becoming very common here; they are now better made and much cheaper than formerly; and the better houses, built within the last seven years, have not the smells about them that the better houses built formerly have. The servants prize them very much, and they will become common for labouring men, where there is a convenience in getting into a common drain. Indeed the water-closets have been built for the servants, in consequence of the servants using those made for their masters, instead of going to their own privy in the yard. Whenever we have fevers in this town, it is generally in those places where the privies are badly kept, and where there is a pool of water stagnant, perhaps, for one-half the year.

Besides provision for drainage in any Building Bill, what other measures do you think require to be provided for compulsorily?
Undoubtedly ventilation; it is even more important than anything I have yet mentioned. Proper arrangements for ventilation may be provided at an expense that is to be considered next to nothing. A good house may be ventilated for a few shillings. Here the poor are badly off for ventilation; they have scarce a sash or a pane that will open, and ventilation flues for cottages are almost unknown. Where people are living in large numbers, the close smell you experience on entering their rooms is extremely oppresive. If the ventilation were duly attended to, I am convinced that far fewer doctors would be needed than now are. I would never have a house built, if it could be avoided, without a flue appropriated for the purpose of ventilation. I venture to say that the execution of such a provision might be very safely left to the discretion of any proper officer.

Have you ever any houses fall down, or is life endangered in this district, from defects in respect to thickness of walls or floors?
I recollect nothing of the kind. Our houses are usually built with stone.

Have you had any failure of public buildings attended with loss of life, which might be evidence of the necessity of legislation in that respect?
None whatever.

When you build cottages, do you carry up the walls above the roof, so as to protect them against fire?
We do; we carry them up to the top because it saves timber; it saves binding; the wall up to the top does not cost half so much as a binding would cost.

APPENDIX C

THE BUILDINGS

c.1802 THORNTON LODGE, Longroyd Bridge, Huddersfield. For John Horsfall.

1811 BROWN COW INN, Market Place, Huddersfield. For Daniel Armitage.

1816-19 HOLY TRINITY CHURCH, Greenhead, Huddersfield. Architect T. Taylor. For Benjamin Haigh Allen.

1818-9 METHODIST CHAPEL, Queen Street, Huddersfield.

c.1818 THE RIDING SCHOOL, Huddersfield.

1823 BARN at Grange Ash. For Sir John Lister Kaye.

1823-26 ST. PAUL'S CHURCH, Shipley. Architect John Oates. For the Church Building Commissioners.

1824-25 INDEPENDENT CHAPEL, Ramsden Street.

1825-27 MILL, Folly Hall. Number one mill.

1827-29 CHRIST CHURCH, Linthwaite. Architect Peter Atkinson. For the Church Building Commissioners.

1827-29 HOLY TRINITY CHURCH, South Crosland. Architect Peter Atkinson. For the Church Building Commissioners.

1828-29 ST. JOHN'S CHURCH, Golcar. Architect Peter Atkinson. For the Church Building Commissioners.

1828-30 ST. STEPHEN'S CHURCH, Lindley. Architect John Oates. For the Church Building Commissioners.

1828-30 ALL SAINT'S CHURCH, Paddock. Architect John Oates. For the Church Building Commissioners.

1828-31 ST. PAUL'S CHURCH, Huddersfield. Architect John Oates. For the Church Building Commissioners.

c.1828-29 ST. PAUL'S CHURCH, Birkenshaw. Architects Messrs Atkinson & Sharp. For the Church Building Commissioners.

1829-31 HUDDERSFIELD & UPPER AGBRIGG INFIRMARY, New North Road. Architect John Oates.

c.1831-32 ST. PATRICK'S CHURCH, Huddersfield. Architect John Child. For the Roman Catholic Church.

1833 MILL, Folly Hall. Number two mill.

c. 1842 WAREHOUSE & HOUSES, Victoria Street, Huddersfield.

c.1844 MILL, Folly Hall. Rebuilding of number one mill following destruction by fire.

1846-47 RAILWAY STATION, Huddersfield. Architect J.P. Pritchett. For the Huddersfield & Manchester Railway & Canal Co and the Huddersfield & Sheffield Junction Railway Co.

1846-47 CART BRIDGE, above Kings Mill, Huddersfield. Two abuttments and two stone piers for a wooden bridge over the River Colne. It was destroyed in the deluge of Holmfirth flood, 1852. For the Ramsden estate.

1848 CLOTH HALL BUTRESSES, Huddersfield. For the Ramsden estate.

1848 FOX STREET, Huddersfield.

1849-51 GEORGE HOTEL, Huddersfield. Architect William Wallen. For the Ramsden estate.

1850 GEORGE HOTEL STABLES, Huddersfield. Architect William Wallen. For the Ramsden estate.

1852 MARKET CROSS, Huddersfield. Re-erection. For Ramsden estate.

1851-52 BRITANNIA BUILDINGS, Huddersfield. Originally known as Crosland's Building. Architect William Cocking. For George Crosland.

1851-53 ST. JOHN'S CHURCH, Bay Hall. Architect William Butterfield. For the Trustees of the will of Sir John Ramsden.

c.1856 MILL, Folly Hall. Rebuilding following fire. Commenced by Kaye, completed by his executors.

SOURCES

GENERAL

The papers of Kaye's executors, which contain draft wills, family detail, valuations, sale particulars etc. and which have been previously utilised by Mrs. E.A. Hilary Haigh in an article Joseph Kaye - a builder of Huddersfield (Old West Riding Vol. 4 No. 1) are at West Yorkshire Archives, Wakefield, C296/136 to 138.

Records of the Ramsden Estate including the rentals and extensive correspondence from which many references have been drawn, are at West Yorkshire Archives, Kirklees.

The indexed memorials of deeds held at the West Riding Registry of Deeds, Wakefield, have provided much information which has not been individually referenced.

References have been drawn from the collection of Huddersfield and Yorkshire Directories held at Huddersfield Central Library, Local History Studies Section.

SPECIFIC

1 Appendix to First Report of the Commissioners of Inquiry into the State of Large Towns and Populous Districts.
2 Kirkheaton Parish Registers, Marriages 10.6.1841.
3 West Yorkshire Archives, Wakefield, QE32/7.
4 Huddersfield Examiner 20.3.1858.
5 Huddersfield Examiner 24.9.1918
6 West Yorkshire Archives, Kirklees KA35
7 Huddersfield Daily Examiner 15.1.1957
8 West Yorkshire Archives, Kirklees KC165/29
9 West Yorkshire Archives, Wakefield, QE2/13/15
10 Huddersfield Chronicle 20.3.1858
11 West Yorkshire Archives, Wakefield C296/90
12 White's Directory 1853
13 West Yorkshire Archives, Kirklees, KC165/29
14 Ibid DD/RE/R
15 West Yorkshire Archives, Wakefield, QE32
16 Huddersfield Central Library, Local History Department
17 West Yorkshire Archives, Wakefield, C296/83
18 Ibid C296/218
19 Huddersfield Central Library, Local History Department.

20 Personal Correspondence, Miss Auty
21 West Riding Registry of Deeds HU/416/385
22 West Yorkshire Archives, Kirklees, T/C/33.
23 West Riding Registry of Deeds SK/58/64
24 West Yorkshire Archives, Kirklees, CH/F
25 Huddersfield Examiner 1.7.1911.
26 West Yorkshire Archives, Wakefield, D32/89.
27 Borthwick Institute, York, July 1791, Pontefract Deanery.
28 Ibid December 1821, Pontefract Deanery.
29 Leeds Mercury 10.6.1837
30 A.W. Sykes, Ramsden Street Chapel, Notes & Records, 1825-1925.
31 Leeds Mercury 30.4.1825
32 Rev. Francis X. Singleton, A Historical Record of St. Patrick's Church, Huddersfield.
33 Huddersfield Chronicle 20.8.1870.
34 West Yorkshire Archives, Wakefield C296/232.
35 West Riding Registry of Deeds IM/485/477
36 West Yorkshire Archives, Kirklees, CH/F.
37 Ibid KC165/38.
38 Ibid KHT/2/1.
39 Ibid DD/RM/23.
40 Yorkshire Archaeological Society MS491.
41 Huddersfield Examiner 20.9.1851, & Huddersfield Chronicle 27.8.1853.
42 Leeds Mercury 7.4.1849.
43 Yorkshire Archaeological Society MD234/326.
44 Huddersfield Central Library, Local History Department, Cuttings - Guild Hall.
45 Ibid Cuttings Book 5.10.1918.